Four Seasons of Joy!

Holly M. Roddam

WestBow Press books may be ordered through booksellers or by contacting:

WestBow Press
A Division of Thomas Nelson & Zondervan
1663 Liberty Drive
Bloomington, IN 47403
www.westbowpress.com
844-714-3454

ISBN: 978-1-6642-3318-8 (sc)
ISBN: 978-1-6642-3319-5 (e)

Library of Congress Control Number: 2021908744

Print information available on the last page.

WestBow Press rev. date: 6/29/2021

WESTBOW
P R E S S®
A DIVISION OF THOMAS NELSON
& ZONDERVAN

Dedication

For Dylan on her 7th birthday.
Thank you for liking my poems and encouraging me to finish the book.
May you have many happy years of reading ahead of you
and maybe even of writing a book or two of your own!!

Peace & Love,
Nana Holly <><

CONTENTS

Spring
Spring Thaw 2
Groundhog Day 4
Spring Flowers 5
The First Signs of Spring 6
Something's Going On 10
Muddle Puddles 12

Summer
Vacation Time 14
Tubing 16
The Ocean's Notion 18
The Pride of the Apple Tree 19
Nana the Gardener 20
Let's Go Fly a Kite 22

Fall
Autumn's Invitation 24
The Pile 26
The Giant's Sneeze 27
Blueberries 28
The Gigantic Pumpkin 30

Winter
When It's Cold Outdoors.. 32
The Joy of Snow 35
Snow 36
The Silly Old Snowman 38
Snowbirds 39

SPRING

Spring Thaw

The ice is melting. Oh, come and see!
The brook is singing it's melody.
Welcoming back the warmth of the sun,
Lifting the spirits of everyone.

The snow is going. 'Tis sad to say.
It gave many hours of fun and play.
Our snowman is shrinking to the ground.
It won't be long 'til he's not around.

The earth is thawing this time of year
It won't be long before spring is here.
Budding plants pop their heads through the snow,
Reminding us of the life below.

The sap is running. Each maple's trunk
Gives up prized liquid with each kerplunk.
Buckets on spigots catch every drop,
Making a symphony plop by plop.

Spring is coming. Oh, can't you tell?
The birds and bees and lovely new smells
Make me so happy I want to shout,
Kick off my shoes and dance about!

Groundhog Day

Every year the groundhog pokes his nose out of the ground.
He looks around to see if his shadow can be found.
And if it can't, he jumps for joy for spring is on its way.
But if he can, he quickly turns and hides himself away.

Six more weeks of winter, if his shadow he does see.
I really hope the sun won't shine so there'll be an early spring!
But even if the shadow's there, I guess that that's okay,
For nothing beats the snow, when you go outside to play.

Spring Flowers

The flowers that bloom in the spring
Would be fit for a queen or a king.
But lucky for me,
In my garden they'll be.
What aroma their fragrance will bring.

The First Signs of Spring

There's nothing quite like the first signs of spring
When the snow finally melts and the birds start to sing.
The little buds push their heads through the earth
For nothing can stop this wondrous rebirth.

There's nothing quite like that very first green
That shimmers and shivers as it wakes from its dream.
As millions of leaves unfold on the trees
That fresh limey hue waves its praise in the breeze.

There's nothing quite like that first thundershower
That waters the grass as the light shows its power.
That long drink poured out spurs each new plant to grow
And refreshes the air as it melts all the snow.

There's nothing quite like the first sign of birds
Making nests in the trees and digging for worms.
Soon little hatchlings will open their beaks
And mother will fill them with live tasty treats.

There's nothing quite like the first flower blooms,
That when plucked from outside, will adorn many rooms.
Or if left in garden will continue to grow
And the whole summer long will put on quite a show.

There's nothing quite like the first signs of spring
When the snow finally melts and the birds start to sing.
The little buds push their heads through the earth
For nothing can stop this wondrous rebirth.

Something's Going On

Come to the barn! There's something going on.
There in the hay, some babes are being born.
Look! The little lambs are learning how to stand.
It doesn't take them long, and no one gave a hand.

The new calf is drinking milk from his mother.
What a smart creation - a cow with an udder!
It's great that cows share their milk with you and me
So we can grow healthy bones and strong, pretty teeth.

The little chicks are hatching and chirping really loud!
They're so soft and fluffy, just like a yellow cloud.
They look like dandelions blowing in the breeze,
Stirring dust around them that almost makes me sneeze!

The barn is really hopping with all this new life
And sometimes, the farmer has to be a midwife.
But whether or not they lend a helping hand
The miracle of new birth shows that spring is in the land.

Muddle Puddles

Have you ever wanted to run and splash
In a big muddle puddle in boots and moustache?
I can't help myself! I get this great urge
To find muddle puddles so my feet can submerge.

I jump and I dance and I sing and I twirl.
The water goes flying with a spray and a swirl.
And my heart soars so high - to the clouds in the sky
With joy - knowing that I don't have to stay dry.

Why not try it this spring, when the snow starts to melt?
Put on your raincoat, your boots and a belt.
Go outside, don't worry, there won't be a fuddle.
Jump in and enjoy your own muddle puddle!

Vacation Time

Very soon, in the month of June,
A thrill starts to build by the light of the moon.
This is the season that's so very pleasin'
All because there's no school!

It's summertime, and the weather is fine.
I don't hesitate to stay out real late
On account that I'll be asleep until three;
There's no need to be up any sooner.

These lazy days leave me lost in a haze.
I relax in the sun, then go for a run.
Maybe I'll fish, or just sit here and wish
That every day could be like this one.

Tubing

My Dad used to tell of a gentle old river
Where he used to go as a child.
In an old rubber tire, he would float by the hour
While his face could do nothing but smile.

I'd like to go tubing down a gentle old river.
I'd even be glad for a stream.
To float like a boat past an old billy goat,
I'm sure it would seem like a dream.

And watching the clouds in the sky up above
Seeing animals, faces and shapes,
Would pass the time well, and give something to tell
Later on, munching handfuls of grapes.

Yes, tubing will be on my list for this summer.
I'll make my best effort to go.
And if I enjoy it, I just might employ it
Next year, with my buddies in tow.

The Ocean's Notion

The unwavering Atlantic Ocean
One day, acknowledged the notion
That the seas were too rough,
Making sailing too tough,
So it made the waves go in slow motion.

The Pride of the Apple Tree

There once was a big apple tree
That shared with a small chickadee
That the pride in his fruit,
Which was really a beaut',
Came from work that was done by a bee!

Nana the Gardener

Nana is a gardener, with prize flowers galore.
She's even won some flower shows. She'll probably win more!
She loves her garden dearly and gives it lots of care,
And sometimes, if I'm very good, she lets me play out there.

She calls it play, but I'm not fooled! She makes me do her work!
By pulling weeds, and digging stones and finding worms that lurk.
We give the plants some water, or they'd shrivel up and die,
And we wear a garden bonnet so the sun's out of our eyes.

And then, at last, my favourite thing, the part I love the best,
The prettiest flowers out there are cut out from the rest.
We take them to the kitchen to arrange them perfectly,
Then take them to a flower show for all the world to see.

Nana's flowers seem to be a cut above the others.
Nana says that's because her garden is her "druthers".
She'd "druther" be out working in the soil with her bare hands
Than any other place on earth, or any foreign lands.

So that's how Nana wins the shows, and why I play along.
I want to learn her gardening skills and learn how to belong
In the world of Nana's garden, where each flower is a friend.
'Cause when I grow up, I want to be just like her, in the end.

Let's Go Fly a Kite

Lately, I've taken to flying a kite.
Each time the wind blows I run with delight.
The kite takes my prayers up into the sky -
Secrets not shared, and what makes me cry.
God takes my prayers, sent on paper and sticks
Offering to smooth all my worldly conflicts,
Forgiving my trespasses, healing my pains,
Loving me always, no matter the stains.
Yellow and red and purple and green
All over the seaside my kite can be seen.
Kissing the clouds and the birds flying by
Invading their space while the eagle flies high.
Tied to my string I feel carried away.
Earth cannot hold me, no, not today.

FALL

Autumn's Invitation

Who's that trampling through my big backyard?
Just your little neighbour
no need to be 'en garde'.

Where are you going on this fine autumn day?
I'm going to the woods
before the leaves blow away.

What will you do with the leaves as they fall?
I'm going to make a mountain
by heaping them tall.

Why would you stack them in such a huge mound?
I want to hear them crackle -
it's such a lovely sound.

How do they crackle just being in a pile?
It's when you jump and roll in them.
It will make you smile!

When can we go? It sounds like lots of fun!
Let's go now, then we can play
until the setting sun!

The Pile

Yellow, gold, orange,
Red leaves in a giant pile.
Inviting me in.

The Giant's Sneeze

There once was a tree full of leaves.
But a giant came by and he sneezed. (Ach-chooo!)
The wind that arose,
Blowing out of his nose,
Made the foliage fly off in the breeze.

Blueberries

Blueberry season comes this time of year.
The berries are ripe and the harvest is here.
I could pick berries for over an hour.
As my bucket gets full I just hope they're not sour!

Highbush blueberry picking is best.
You can pick standing up, that I'll never protest!
The blueberries grow like grapes on a vine,
Come off by the handful, and taste mighty fine!

I have to admit, lowbush berries taste great.
Growing close to the ground, they are picked with a rake.
They take longer to pick than the big highbush blues,
But it's worth it if they are the ones that you choose.

Some berries are sour, Some berries are sweet.
Some are for pies, and some you just eat!
Blueberries are good nutritionally too,
But that's not why I eat them. I just love them, don't you?

The Gigantic Pumpkin

There once was a gigantic pumpkin,
That was carved by the local town bumpkin.
He created a boat.
And it really did float!
So he put out to sea as he jumped in.

When It's Cold Outdoors

When it's cold outdoors, that's when I just might
Grab a good book and some tasty delight.
A grilled cheese perhaps, or some soup in a mug,
Then curl up by the fire like a bug in a rug.

After walking home with the wind at my back,
Some hot apple cider and nuts for a snack
Warm my heart and my soul, right down to my toes,
While the steam from my cup thaws my poor frozen nose.

At bedtime, having spent a day in the snow,
A cup of hot chocolate and a shortbread will go
A very long way to settling my tummy.
How could they not? They are really quite yummy!

The best winter treats come when Christmas draws nigh-
Gingerbread houses, two feet high!
Egg nog, candy canes, and peppermint bark,
Boxes of chocolate - the light and the dark.

I really don't mind when it's cold outdoors.
I can stay in exploring what's hidden in drawers.
Or build a big tent out of blankets and chairs,
Or hide out with cookies under the stairs.

When it's cold outside, there's so much to eat.
I told you what I like. What's your favourite treat?

The Joy of Snow

Some people say, "Oh snow! Go away!
You make life too hard to play!"
But I want you to know,
This white stuff called "snow",
Makes for hours of fun and I want it to stay!

Snow

Snowballs, snowball fights,
forts made of snow.
Tunnels and igloos
to protect from the foe.

Snow angels, snow sculptures,
snow people too.
Snowsuits with mittens,
scarves and snowshoes.

Freshly fallen snow,
catching snow on our tongues.
Dancing ice crystals,
icy air in our lungs.

Hanging ice spears from the roof of the house
Dripping droplets of water as quiet as a mouse.

It's really no wonder I love snow this way.
For all of its blessings so easily outweigh
The fact that it's cold, and I must wear warm dress.
It's my favourite season, I have to confess.

The Silly Old Snowman

There once was a silly old snowman
Who devised a ridiculous game plan.
He would sit in the breeze
And hope he would freeze
While the sun toasted him to a deep tan.

Snowbirds

Believe it or not, there are places on earth
Where winter is sunny - say, Orlando or Perth.
But I can't imagine a winter that's warm
Because where I come from that isn't the norm!

I've heard that some folks like to fly to the sun
And hide away there 'til the winter is done.
They call themselves "Snowbirds", but I'm not one of those.
I'll take the cold days 'til they freeze off my toes!

Printed in the United States
by Baker & Taylor Publisher Services